BEST OF
OXFORD

POSUI DEUM ADIUTOREM MEUM

EST REPOSITA JUSTITIÆ CO

PRÆSIDE THOMA TURNER

UNICHROME

BEST OF
OXFORD

CONTENTS

Written and edited by Rachel Minay.
The author has asserted her moral rights.
Designed by Simon Borrough.
Front cover designed by John Buckley.
The publishers would like to thank Jane Curran, Oxford Blue Badge Guide, for reading the text.
ISBN 1 871004 84 5   1/01

FS32611
Pitkin Unichrome is a publishing, design and photo-graphic company registered to ISO 9001 by the British Standards Institution.

Acknowledgements:
Photography by John Heseltine. Additional photography by kind permission of the following:
Ashmolean Museum of Art and Archaeology, University of Oxford: 38BR; *The Bate Collection of Musical Instruments, University of Oxford:* 47B; *Matt Brown:* 49TL; *Cogges Manor Farm Museum:* 58; *Collections:* 50 (Robert Harding Picture Library), 59TL (John Heseltine Archive), 35TL&B, 36TL, 51B, 57B, 60C, 62 (all by Oxford Picture Library/ Chris Andrews); *Giles Hudson © Museum of the History of Science, Oxford, Image no. 150855:* 16T; *Kelmscott Manor:* 59BL (Reproduced with the permission of the Society of the Antiquaries of London); *Derek Meacock:* 31L, 37; *Madge Meacock:* 30B; *Chris Minay:* 26BL (Reproduced with the permission of the Warden and Fellows of Merton College, Oxford), 34, 35TR, 36TR, 52B, 57TL&R, 59R, 60T&B, 63T, BL&BR; *Tony Nutley/Carlton TV:* 45B; *The Oxford Story:* 17T; *Oxford United Football Club:* 38BL; *Oxfordshire County Council Photographic Archive:* 11B; *Pitkin Unichrome:* 18BL, 23BR, 56 (Heather Hook), 61 (Heather Hook); *Pitt Rivers Museum, University of Oxford:* 40L.

INTRODUCTION

The origins of Oxford, like the city today, are a subtle blend of town and gown. Here oxen forded a river, a Saxon princess founded a monastery and a world-famous university was born. Some have been born and bred in the city, many more have been drawn to it over the years – to learn, to work, to be inspired. Oxford has seen battles, romances, industry and poetry. The university has been criticized from within the city for the role it has played in the lives of the townspeople, and from without for being too elitist and slow to change. Yet it has provided Oxford with some of its most breathtaking architecture and an outstanding reputation. Oxford may always be criticized. It will also always be admired and loved.

The sheer size of Christ Church's breathtaking Tom Quad reflects the scale of Thomas Wolsey's vision for 'Cardinal College'. Wolsey completed three-quarters of the quad before he fell from power: the final side (a faithful copy of his work) and the splendid Tom Tower were added in the 17th century.

THE ORIGINS OF OXFORD

There is evidence of neolithic settlement around Oxford. Stone arrowheads have been found in Christ Church Meadow and stone tools discovered elsewhere. There seems to have been more settlement in the Bronze Age, borne out by suggestions of barrows on Port Meadow and a barrow cemetery in the University Parks. Unlike York or Chester, Oxford did not signify under the Romans, except perhaps as a centre of pottery manufacture. The real beginnings of Oxford lie in the Saxon period when a princess and nun, Frideswide, founded a monastery here in the 8th century. The site of Frideswide's monastery was to be the site of Christ Church Cathedral.

SAXON OXFORD

Oxford increased in importance and prosperity enormously during the Saxon period. The town was well placed on the boundary of two kingdoms – Wessex and Mercia – on a trade route and near a river crossing. Furthermore it had a monastery, boosting prosperity and encouraging stability.

In the 9th century King Alfred had initiated a political and administrative system designed to keep the Danes at bay. In 911 Edward the Elder, Alfred's son, gave Oxford royal protection and fortification. The Saxon tower of St Michael at the North Gate that survives to this day, was just that – a part of the north gate.

Dating from about 1030, the Saxon tower of St Michael at the North Gate is Oxford's oldest building.

In 1002 there was a horrific massacre of the Danes in Oxford. King Ethelred the Unready had ordered that all Danes should be put to death. The Danish men, women and children fled into Frideswide's monastery and it was burned to the ground with the people inside. Sweyn Forkbeard, the king of Denmark, attacked England in revenge and Oxford was sacked by Thorkell the Tall in 1009. The ravaged monastery was rebuilt as the Augustinian Priory of St Frideswide over 100 years later.

NORMAN OXFORD

In 1071 Robert d'Oilly, a Norman governor who had fought with William the Conquerer at the Battle of Hastings, built a castle in Oxford. The Empress Matilda was held captive there in 1142, during the civil war of King Stephen's reign. It is said that she escaped by camouflaging herself in a white sheet and thus was not seen fleeing across the frozen river and away. In 1215 the Barons trapped King John in the castle – they would later force him to sign Magna Carta at Runnymede. All that remains of the castle today is an artificial earth mound and St George's Tower, probably the tallest of a number of towers built into the bailey.

Robert d'Oilly also established an Augustinian priory to the west. This building developed into Oseney Abbey, in its time one of the largest abbeys in England.

MEDIEVAL OXFORD

During the Middle Ages much of the wealth created in Oxford went to religious houses, the number of which increased as the town became more prosperous. Godstow Nunnery, the ruins of which survive today, was founded in 1133.

These religious institutions laid the foundations for Oxford to become a place of learning: by the 12th century there was a medieval university for the scholarship of clerics. By early in the 13th century the town's reputation had grown and was drawing more people. The Dominicans established a friary in 1221, the Franciscans in 1224, and the Carmelites in 1256. An abbey was founded for the Cistercians in 1280 and a college for the Benedictines in 1283. The friars' students lived and worked in academic halls, most of which disappeared as they were replaced by the colleges. Beam Hall in cobbled Merton Street is one that has survived as student accommodation.

St George's Tower narrows towards the top and the walls at the base are 2.7 metres (9 feet) thick.

'Fair Rosamund', the mistress of Henry II, was buried at Godstow Nunnery in 1175. According to legend, Rosamund was murdered by Queen Eleanor, but the truth may be that she retired to Godstow when she was no longer a favourite with the king.

The Black Death of 1348 hit Oxford hard. While the colleges could remove their scholars to country locations, the townspeople had no such privilege. As the local population declined, the university gained control of more land in the town. Resentment about the dominance of the university in the governing of the town had been brewing for some time and there had been a rash of riots in the 13th century. However, the most notorious clash between 'town and gown' was in 1355 – the St Scholastica's Day riot. Some university clerks had been drinking in the Swyndlestock Tavern, close to Carfax, (a sign on the current Abbey National building indicates the site of the tavern). They argued with the vintner about the quality of the wine and threw the wine at his head. The townsfolk were insulted and rallied the people from St Martin's church while the students did the same from St Mary's. The fighting was bloody and lasted for three days. Over 60 students were killed, but the university had won. In atonement the mayor and 63 citizens had to swear allegiance to the chancellor of the university and pay a penny for each of the murdered scholars. The penance stopped with the Civil War but the church attendance continued until 1825.

By the end of the 14th century, eight of the colleges we know today had been founded: University, Merton, Balliol, Exeter, St Edmund Hall, Oriel, The Queen's and New College.

Carfax Tower is all that remains of St Martin's Church which stood at the crossroads until the 19th century. The name 'Carfax' is generally thought to come from the latin quadrifurcus *meaning 'four forks'.*

THE REFORMATION AND 16TH-CENTURY OXFORD

As a centre of monastic life, the town was vastly altered as a result of the Reformation. The religious buildings that represented the beginnings of the university were destroyed in the Dissolution of the Monasteries. Henry VIII's patronage ensured that the university would survive, but also marked a change in teaching, moving away from monastic learning and towards more secular subjects.

The former New Inn on the corner of Cornmarket Street and Ship Street dates from the late 14th century. This charming timber-framed building has been carefully restored. The façade consists of three storeys with each storey 'jettied' out over the one below.

Queen Mary's ascension to the throne spelt the fate of the Protestant Bishops Hugh Latimer and Nicholas Ridley and Archbishop Thomas Cranmer, who came to be known as the Oxford Martyrs. The three men were imprisoned first at the Golden Cross Inn and then at the Bocardo prison. The door of the cell in which they were held in the Bocardo can be seen in the tower of St Michael at the North Gate. Tried and found guilty of heresy, they were burned at the stake at a point now marked with a simple cross on the surface of Broad Street.

CAPITAL OF THE CIVIL WAR

During the English Civil War Oxford acted as the headquarters of Charles I and the Royalists. From 1642–46 Charles lodged at Christ Church and Queen Henrietta Maria stayed at Merton – the rooms she lodged in are still called the Queen's Rooms. Although the town was predominantly Parliamentarian, support for the king was high in the university. The influx of people placed a burden on Oxford: there were outbreaks of plague and typhus, and in 1644 a great fire destroyed a quarter of the city.

The Puritans entered Oxfordshire in 1645 and the surrender treaty was signed at Christ Church on 20 June 1646. Oliver Cromwell was made chancellor of the university in 1650 and some of the colleges acquired new heads with more sympathy for the Parliamentary cause.

It is said that scholars fought among themselves or against others so often and with such force, that blood has flowed on every inch of pavement between Carfax and St Mary's.

During the 16th century the medieval Cross Inn was frequented by groups of travelling players. In 1593 a production of Hamlet was performed in the courtyard of the Golden Cross, now a beautifully-restored enclave of boutiques and eateries.

Oxford was the Royalist capital during the English Civil War. The inscription above the staircase in Oriel's Front Quad reads Regnante Carolo – 'When Charles reigns'.

18TH-CENTURY ARCHITECTURE AND 19TH-CENTURY EXPANSION

The 18th century heralded the arrival of some of Oxford's most beautiful landmarks, in particular the sublime Radcliffe Camera, a round library that fits perfectly into a square space. Other building projects included the Radcliffe Observatory, the rebuilding of The Queen's College and Nicholas Hawksmoor's Clarendon Building.

At the end of the 18th century the canal reached Oxford from Coventry and about 50 years later the railway arrived. The population of the city quadrupled from just under 12,000 to just under 50,000 during the 19th century. The strain that this placed on local government resulted in the creation of the Oxford Local Board in 1865 and the unification of day and night police in 1868.

Changes were also happening in the social and cultural arenas. In 1811 Percy Shelley, an undergraduate at University College, was sent down for writing 'The Necessity of Atheism'. In the 1830s the Oxford Movement was born, led by John Keble, Edward Pusey and the charismatic John Newman. The Movement supported a High Church or 'catholic' (but not Roman Catholic) church. Newman himself became a Roman Catholic in 1845, an event which had an enormous effect on

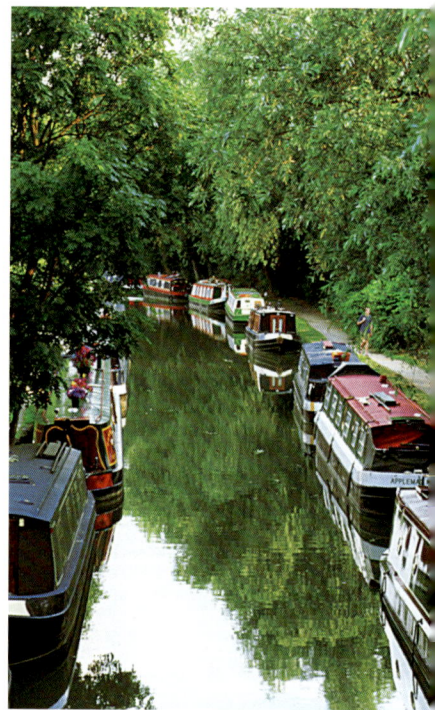

A tranquil scene of colourful narrowboats framing the canal at Jericho. A walk or cycle along the towpath provides an escape from the busy city.

the people of his day. As new religious groups formed, the university's role began to be questioned and eventually developed a greater emphasis on the study of science. In the arena of the Arts, the Pre-Raphaelite movement began at Exeter College where William Morris and Edward Burne-Jones were undergraduates. And by 1880 women were admitted to university lectures, although they would not be able to receive degrees for another 40 years. The women's academic halls that were founded in the late 19th century were not recognized as colleges until 1959–60.

Somerville College was founded in 1879 specifically for the education of women and took its name from Mary Somerville, a Scottish scientific writer and suffragette.

OXFORD FROM MOTORS TO THE MILLENNIUM

The carmaker William R. Morris began his career repairing bicycles in the shed behind his family home in James Street, East Oxford. From repairing he progressed to building and moved to premises at no. 48 High Street. From there he moved on to motorized bicycles and then to repairing motor cars. In 1913, Morris built a car of his own – the Morris Oxford or 'Bullnose' Morris. The cars were assembled in the suburb of Cowley where the factory kept on expanding to meet the demand for his mass-produced cars.

William R. Morris in a 'Bullnose' Morris – the name derives from the car's rounded radiator.

The booming motor industry protected Oxford from the 1930s depression felt elsewhere, but declined in the second half of the 20th century. The growth of service industries in the shape of hospitals and the polytechnic (now Oxford Brookes University) and hi-tech industries helped to combat the decline of motor industry jobs.

The crossroads at the centre of Oxford was busy and congested for centuries. The medieval open-air market that hampered the flow of traffic was moved in the late 18th century. At the end of the following century the church of St Martin, with the exception of the tower, was destroyed. And as Oxford approached the Millennium in 1999, and the traffic pollution was reaching severe levels, the area was closed to all traffic except buses and taxis and Cornmarket Street and Broad Street were partially reclaimed for pedestrians.

The municipal power that the university had for centuries only dissolved in 1974 when the university-elected city councillors were finally abolished from the City Council.

The landmark at the heart of Oxford is St Martin's Tower, or Carfax Tower as it is known. St Martin's Church stood at the crossroads from 1032 until the 19th century when all but the 13th-century west tower was demolished. Dominant as you approach the centre from the High Street, Carfax is not one of the loftiest towers and just registers on Oxford's skyline. In the 14th century the height of the tower was increased and then lowered following complaints from the university about the arrows and stones that people were hurling from the top during clashes between town and gown.

The two soldiers that strike the quarter hour below the clock on Carfax Tower are replicas of the originals which can now be seen in the Museum of Oxford.

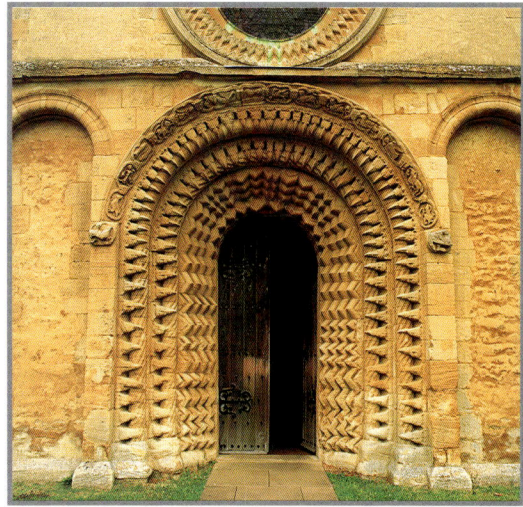

The remains of Oxford castle are not the only legacy of Norman Oxford. The church of St Mary the Virgin, Iffley, is one of the best-preserved and most engaging Norman churches in England. The rose window at the west end dates from the mid-19th century, but the remainder originates from about 1180. The west door may have been used for ceremonial occasions and is strikingly framed by an elaborate zigzag and beakhead style. The linked reliefs above depict signs of the zodiac and symbols of the evangelists.

The earliest weather records in Europe were kept at Merton College in the 14th century.

While there is some debate over which is the oldest college in Oxford, Merton, founded in 1264, was the first college built for the purpose of housing and educating students. It certainly houses Oxford's oldest quad: Mob Quad dates from the 14th century. Small groups of people can enjoy a guided tour of the lovely medieval library, which has a 14th-century reading stall with some books still chained.

The gardens at New College are framed by a considerable length of Oxford's well-preserved old city wall. The original timber wall was replaced in the 12th century and the college became responsible for its maintenance.

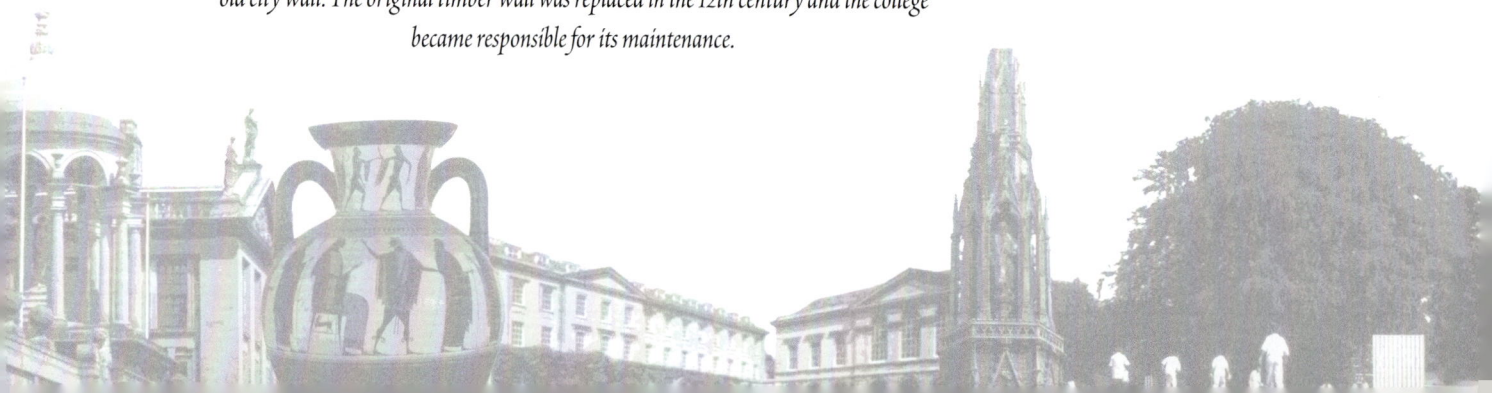

The Museum of Oxford occupies the building that was the former public library and presents a clear history of the city from prehistoric times. The exhibits include reconstructions of period rooms such as a Jericho kitchen and North Oxford drawing room and a skeleton of Giles Covington, a 22-year-old man hanged for murder in the 18th century.

Just around the corner from the Martyrs' Memorial is a cross in the centre of the paving of Broad Street. It is said to mark the spot where Ridley, Latimer and Cranmer were burned in a ditch outside the city walls. There is also a plaque, opposite the cross, on the wall of Balliol College.

When the Catholic Queen Mary came to the throne, the Protestants Cranmer, Latimer and Ridley were tried for heresy and later executed. Latimer and Ridley were burned at the stake in October 1555. Before Cranmer was put to death he retracted the seven recantations he had signed. Having sworn to punish the hand that had written the recantation first, Cranmer thrust his right hand into the flames before he was consumed by the fire. The Martyrs' Memorial, depicting statues of the Oxford Martyrs, was designed by George Gilbert Scott and built in 1841.

The Bocardo prison, where Cranmer was held, was situated above the north gate until 1771. The archbishop was probably forced to watch the execution of Latimer and Ridley from St Michael's tower.

The Museum of the History of Science was built in the early 1680s to house Elias Ashmole's collection of curiosities as well as provide a space for the teaching of science. Today, the museum has a superb collection of historic scientific objects, including sundials, early mathematical and optical instruments, photographic equipment and the largest collection of astrolabes (instruments formerly used in astronomy and navigation) in the world. This 14th-century Middle Gothic astrolabe is of a type written about by Geoffrey Chaucer.

The writer and art critic John Ruskin was educated at Oxford and was one of the supporters of the University Museum, begun in 1855 with the aim of showing the history of life on earth. John Hungerford Pollen, a former Oxford don and decorative artist, designed the entrance porch to the Gothic structure. Pollen's designs depicted Adam, Eve and the Angel of Life – ironic, considering this was the new museum for the natural sciences. The design was only partly carried out with some sections abandoned, and some not even begun.

In 1874 Ruskin organized his students – including Oscar Wilde – to work on a road-building programme in North Hinksey to demonstrate the pleasure and importance of physical work.

During the English Civil War, the university supported the Royalist cause and King Charles made Oxford his headquarters. The Royal Mint was brought to New Inn Hall Street and silver plate from the colleges was melted down to turn into coins. This scene is from The Oxford Story, a journey through the sights and sounds of historic Oxford.

Worcester College was founded in 1714 but stands on the site of Gloucester Hall, a Benedictine establishment founded in 1283. The hall's original medieval cottages and the college's neoclassical 18th-century buildings exist in harmony in the beauty of Worcester College Gardens, a park complete with its own lake.

CATHEDRAL AND COLLEGES

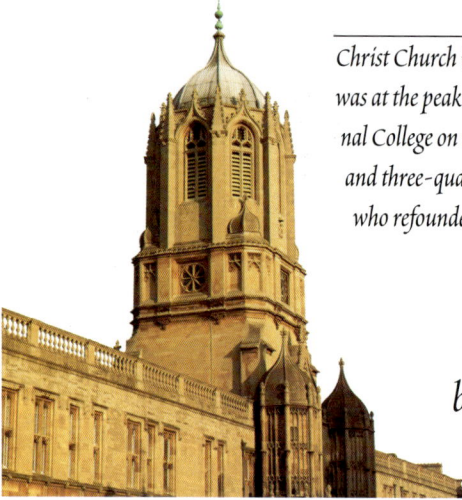

Christ Church is the grandest of all the colleges and it has the largest quad. When Cardinal Thomas Wolsey was at the peak of his career, he determined to build a college on an enormous scale and founded it as Cardinal College on the site of Frideswide's priory. Having completed the Great Hall with its hammerbeam roof and three-quarters of Tom Quad, Wolsey fell from power and the project was taken over by Henry VIII, who refounded it as King Henry VIII's College in 1532. Christ Church received its present name in 1546 when the priory became a cathedral and was united with the college.

Christ Church is never referred to as Christ Church College but its members traditionally refer to it as 'The House' after its Latin name Aedes Christi – the House of Christ.

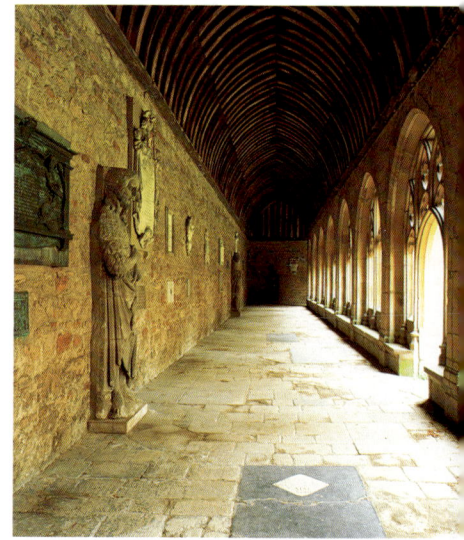

Quiet and magnificent, the cloister at New College is a place to reflect and remember the college's medieval beginnings. The chapel has a 19th-century reredos filled with statues of martyrs, apostles and saints and a hammer-beam roof by George Gilbert Scott.

The astonishing 15th-century interior of the Divinity School is considered to be one of the finest in the country and reflects the importance that was attached to the study of theology. The vaulted ceiling was added in 1480–83 and is adorned with ornamental bosses representing biblical subjects, coats of arms, foliage and animals.

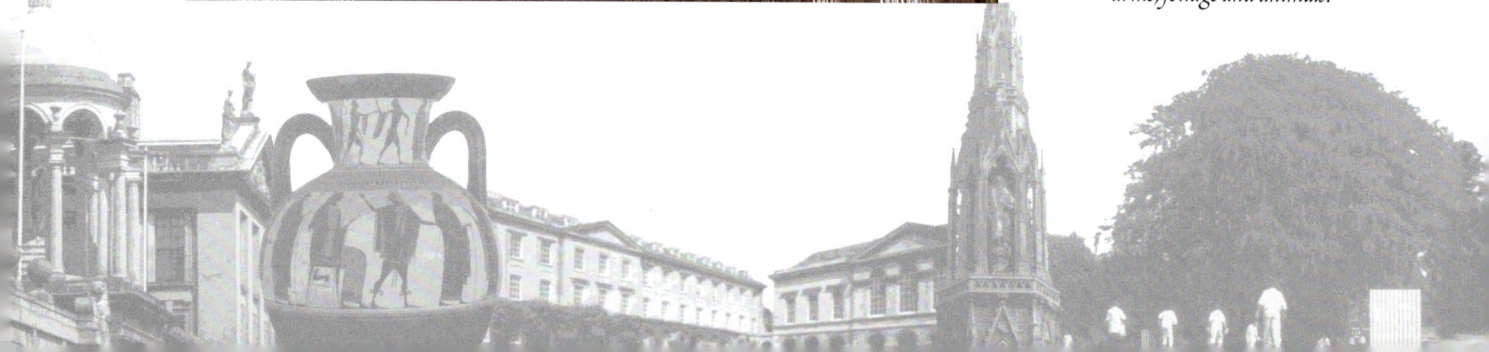

The graduate college of All Souls was founded in 1438 as a memorial to those who died in the Hundred Years' War and it is a beautiful and dignified testament. The twin towers in the remarkable North Quad were designed by Hawksmoor and the large sundial displaying the college emblem is the work of Christopher Wren, who was made a Fellow of the college in 1653.

Magdalen (pronounced 'maudlin') College was founded in 1458. The Hall was one of the earliest buildings, begun in 1474, and restored in 1903 with a copy of the original low-pitched roof.

The full title of Oriel College is 'The Provost and Scholars of the House of the Blessed Mary the Virgin in Oxford, commonly called Oriel College, of the foundation of Edward the Second of famous memory, sometime King of England.'

Oriel Chapel is charming in its austerity. The Gothic windows frame stained glass that includes an early 16th-century figure of St Margaret and a dragon. It was at Oriel that the leaders of the Oxford Movement – Newman, Keble and Pusey – were all Fellows.

The Old Schools Quadrangle, now part of the Bodleian Library, was begun in 1613 and by the end of the century was the headquarters of the university. Beneath the rooftop battlements and pinnacles, the schools included Moral Philosophy, Metaphysics, and Logic on the ground floor, Law, Rhetoric, and Anatomy and Medicine on the first. A bronze statue of William Herbert, the 3rd Earl of Pembroke, stands at the west end. A patron of the arts, Shakespeare's First Folio was dedicated to him and his brother and a college was named after him.

In medieval times, dozens of academic halls with names like Ape Hall and Sparrow Hall were dotted around the town. St Edmund Hall, or Teddy Hall, is the only one of the former halls to survive as a college. The 17th-century Front Quad is small and charming and the church of St Peter in the East, now the college library, has a fine Norman crypt. Visitors can ask at the porter's lodge for access to the crypt and to see the Burne-Jones and Morris stained glass in the chapel.

William Laud, Archbishop of Canterbury from 1633, was president of St John's College from 1611. He was favoured by Charles I and Henrietta Maria, and the highly decorated Canterbury Quad which he financed features their statues. The Quad leads to the spacious gardens.

The Queen's College was named after Queen Philippa of Hainault, consort to Edward III, as its founder, Robert de Eglesfield, was her chaplain. However it is Queen Caroline whose statue adorns the gatehouse, because she supplied funds towards the 18th-century rebuilding programme. This work, which replaced all the original buildings, was for many years attributed to Hawksmoor, but it is now thought to be that of the local mason William Townsend.

Oxford's colleges may have their own decided personalities, but on a superficial level, Keble is the most obviously distinctive. Its mighty neo-Gothic brick façade looms proudly up from Parks Road. In 1892 a side chapel was added to the immense main chapel to house Holman Hunt's The Light of the World.

St John's is one of Oxford's richest colleges: at one time you could travel from St John's in Oxford to St John's in Cambridge without leaving St John's land.

The magnificent Examination Schools were created when it became clear that students could no longer be tested in the Divinity School and Old Schools Quadrangle. Designed by T.G. Jackson, the neo-Jacobean edifice looks intimidating from the High Street and glorious from Merton Street. The building is surprisingly light and airy inside.

Pembroke College can be seen to have suffered for living in the shadow of the noble and wealthy Christ Church, but one of its gems is the richly-coloured chapel. The chapel dates from the early 18th century but the jewel-like wall and ceiling paintings were added in 1884 by the Pre-Raphaelite follower C.E. Kempe. Another of the college's treasures is the teapot belonging to Pembroke's most famous son, Samuel Johnson. One of the greatest intellects ever to have graced Oxford, Johnson was forced to leave without a degree due to lack of funds, but was later made an honorary Master of Arts in respect of his services to literature.

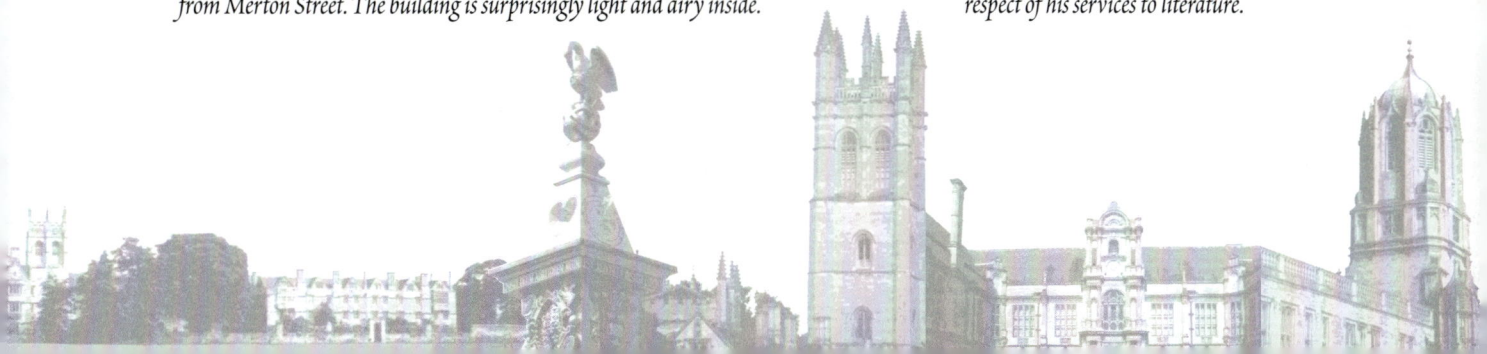

The focal point of St Aldates is the magnificent gate tower known as Tom Tower. Wren built the octagonal tower and cupola to house the bell, Great Tom, which was cast in 1680 to replace the original bell that came from Oseney Abbey. Great Tom still tolls 101 times every night at 9.05, symbolizing the original number of students and the time by which they should be back in college. The precise number of minutes after the hour represents the fact that Oxford is five minutes behind Greenwich Mean Time.

The distinctive sound of Great Tom is an intrinsic part of the music of Oxford: it is said that the bell was muffled during World War I in case its tolling guided zeppelins to the city.

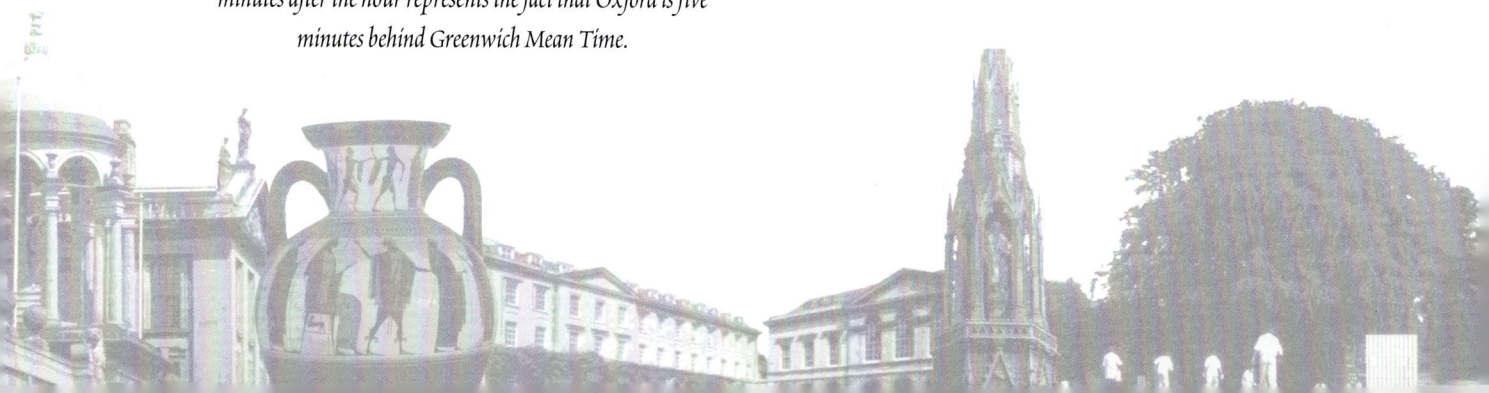

A significant part of the High Street's distinctive skyline, the ornate tower of St Mary's provides a superb view over the heart of the university. The other lofty viewpoints in the city centre are Carfax Tower, the Tower of St Michael at the North Gate and the rooftop cupola of the Sheldonian Theatre.

Perhaps the most impressive aspect of Lincoln College's architecture is the library, converted from the former All Saints Church. Deemed unsafe in the 1660s, the church spire actually collapsed in 1700 and was rebuilt, partly to Hawksmoor's designs. The new tower complements elegant Turl Street and the profound sweep of the High.

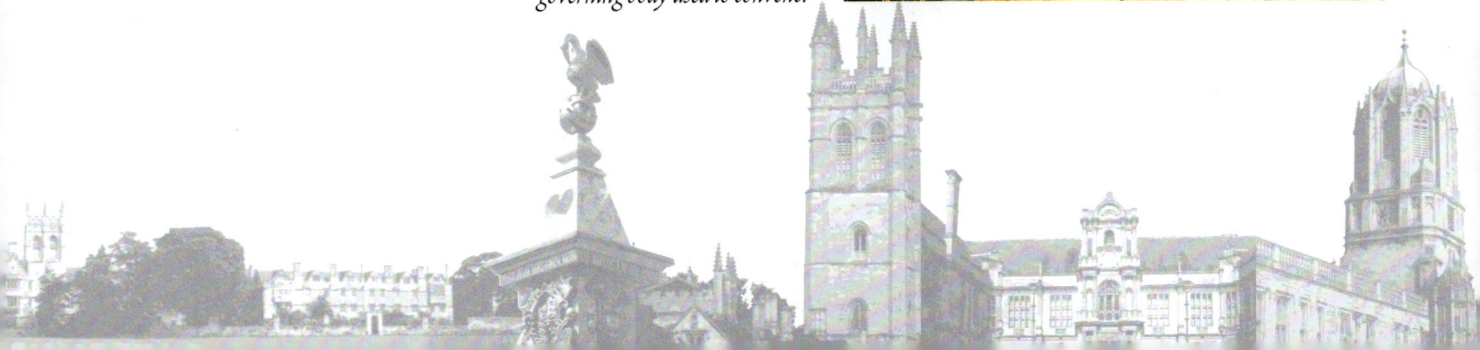

The ties between Oxford University and the imposing church of St Mary the Virgin stretch far into the past, to a time when St Mary's was used for degree ceremonies and trials. The present building is largely 15th and 16th century, but there has been a church on the same site since Saxon times. The south porch, designed by Nicholas Stone and built in 1637, is an example of English Baroque. The Convocation Coffee House inhabits the area in which the university's governing body used to convene.

Neither a spire nor a tower, the Radcliffe Camera is perhaps the most memorable feature in Oxford's skyline and the architectural heart of the university.

Hawksmoor proposed the domed circular form, but James Gibbs was the architect responsible for the final masterpiece.

Originally an independent library, rather than part of the university, the Camera (meaning 'chamber') is now a private reading room for the Bodleian.

Magdalen College choir was so renowned at one time that one choirmaster supposedly dragged a reluctant country boy with an exceptional voice back to Oxford in chains.

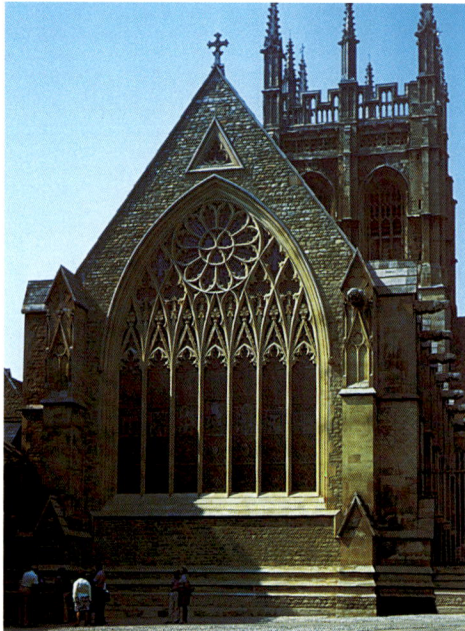

It is thought that Merton chapel tower was built during the 14th century and that by 1450 the exterior of the chapel looked much as it does today. The chapel's interior is particularly fine with exquisite stained glass, and with excellent acoustics is used for many concerts.

The Tower of the Five Orders in the Old Schools Quadrangle gets its name from the tiers of columns adorning its front. These are decorated in the five orders of classical styles: Tuscan, Doric, Ionic, Corinthian and Composite.

If you are familiar with Oxford, then you are familiar with Magdalen's Bell Tower, and yet it never fails to be breathtaking. Begun in 1492 and completed in 1509, this lovely Gothic building has graced the city for nearly five centuries. On May Morning, the choir sing an invocation to summer in Latin from the top of the tower while town and gown celebrate in the streets below.

Physically and aesthetically distanced from Oxford's other dreaming spires, there is something frank and solid about the tower of Nuffield College. William Morris, Lord Nuffield, funded the construction of this postgraduate college with the aim of furthering cooperation between industry and academia.

Cornmarket Street is Oxford's main shopping street and in 1999 was made pedestrian-only in an attempt to combat the problems created by a small city centre coupled with a high volume of traffic.

At one time there was a lead roof over part of Cornmarket Street, but during the English Civil War this was dragged down to be converted into bullets.

An earlier instance of pedestrianizing the city centre was the creation of Gloucester Green in 1989. This square is the setting for the weekly open-air or 'Wednesday' market and the smaller fleamarket every Thursday.

Georgian and Regency architecture can be found in the broad, tree-lined street of St Giles and in nearby Beaumont Street, St John's Street and the charming Beaumont Buildings. For two days in September, the street is closed, traffic is diverted and St Giles' Fair takes over – people, stalls, bright lights and fast rides.

Blackwell's is one of the world's best-known bookshops. The original shop was so small – 3.6m (12ft) square – that it could not comfortably hold more than three customers at a time. Given the size of Blackwell's today, this fact is hard to accept – never more so than in the Norrington Room, an immense underground expanse stacked wall to wall with books of every kind.

Turl Street, or the Turl, is one of Oxford's older, attractive streets and contains some fine buildings as well as Jesus, Exeter and Lincoln Colleges. Its name is thought to derive from a turnstile or 'twirling' gate that once stood in the city wall at the Broad Street end.

A wintry day on Brasenose Lane conjures up the feeling that time in Oxford has stood still. With its central cobbled gulley marking the route of the original open sewer, the lane leads to Radcliffe Square and Brasenose College. The college is so named because of a bronze door knocker (the 'brazen nose') that used to hang on the gates and now hangs in the dining hall.

Halley's comet appears on the famous Bayeux Tapestry – it would have been visible in February 1066. The comet represents an omen of misfortune for King Harold.

The house of Edmund Halley, the great 18th-century astronomer, can only be viewed from the outside, but there is a plaque on the front and the observatory that he built on the roof survives to this day. Halley will always be remembered for his work on the famous comet that bears his name. He only saw the comet once in his lifetime, in 1682, but was convinced that the same comet had appeared before, calculated its orbit and predicted its return.

The picturesque cobbled alley of Bath Place twists and turns to the Turf Tavern, a popular pub with a large attractive beer garden.

High Street, or the High, is something special – boasting some of the finest buildings Oxford can offer, displayed over a long and graceful curve. With the exception of buses and taxis – and of course bicycles – traffic is now diverted along Longwall Street and although some traders have complained about loss of business, clearer streets and cleaner air are probably the benefits to visitors and locals.

The Covered Market that we see today dates from the 1890s and stepping inside can be like stepping back in time. The butchers' shops drip with meat and game, there are colourful florists and grocers, lively cafés and speciality shops to tempt the many passers-by.

Oxford is not just a city of insular university life. The Cowley Road represents a cosmopolitan mix of students and locals and is a jumble of restaurants, pubs, food, junk and New Age shops.

Oxford's Cowley Road saw the birth of bands Radiohead and Supergrass.

The terraced houses of Jericho were built for the workers of the nearby canal, Oxford University Press and ironworks factory. In the past, Jericho – Jude the Obscure's Beersheba – had a reputation for squalor and seediness. Now it is one of Oxford's most popular and fashionable communities, embracing an arthouse cinema, a Raymond Blanc brasserie and characterful pubs like the Bookbinders Arms, one of Inspector Morse's haunts.

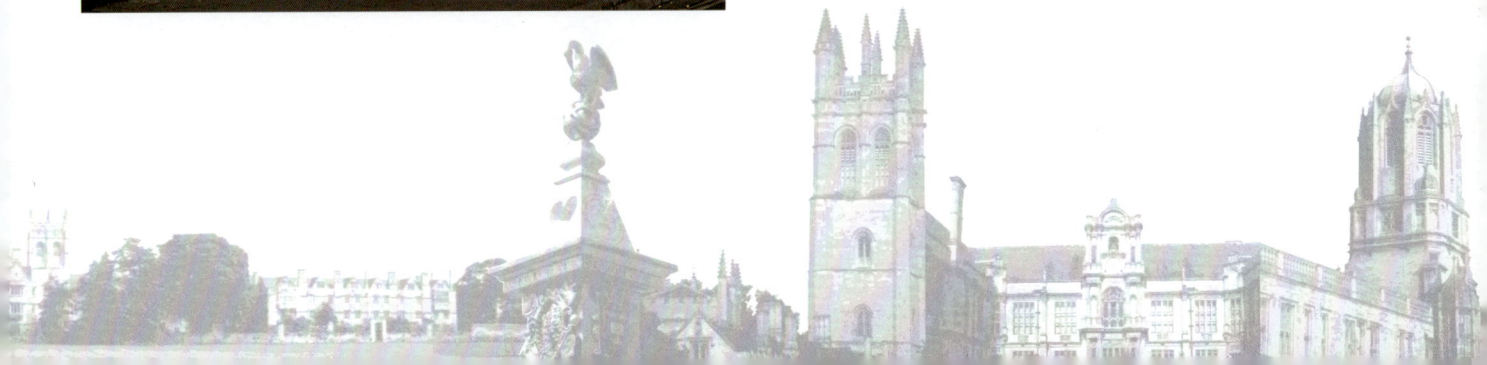

*The river can look at its most magical after a
particularly cold snap. The walk known as
Mesopotamia (from the Greek meaning 'between
the rivers') wends its narrow way between two
strands of the Cherwell.*

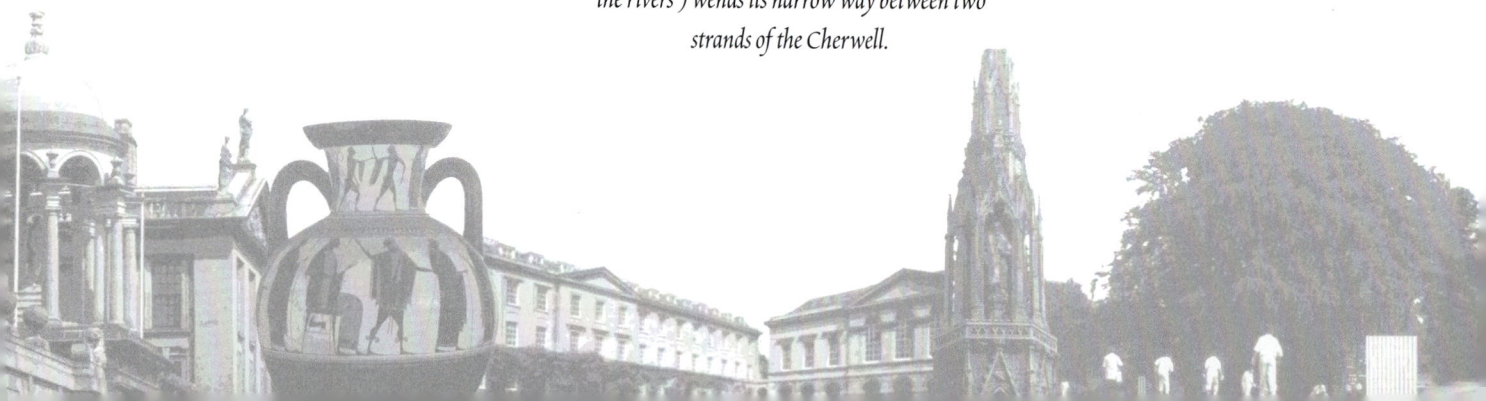

One of Oxford's enduring traditions is the sport of rowing. Torpids is held during the spring term and Eights Week during the summer term. Pictured above is the Wolfson College ladies eights rowing team during Torpids.

The exclusive crescent of Park Town lies under a heavy fall of snow. Much of the architecture in affluent North Oxford is showy Victorian Gothic whereas Park Town (1850–53) is more reminiscent of Regency Bath or London. It still has its Victorian post box.

At the end of Trinity term, students dress up in black tie, dinner jackets and ball gowns to attend their 'Commemoration Balls' – opulent occasions with fine food, champagne and partying till dawn.

In spring, crowds fill the centre of Oxford to celebrate the old tradition of May Morning. The college choir sings a Latin grace from the top of Magdalen Tower at 6 a.m., morris men dance, and everyone else enjoys beer and breakfast. These morris men are dancing in front of the Clarendon Building, built for the Oxford University Press but now housing part of the collection of the Bodleian Library.

The Encaenia ceremony takes place during June. Members of the university dress up in traditional regalia and process through the streets before bestowing honorary degrees on visiting dignitaries.

There has been a two-day fair held in St Giles since at least the early 17th century. Although the modern fair is a bewildering blend of loud music and stomach-churning rides, traditional amusements like the galloping horses have enduring popularity.

The gardens of Magdalen College in summer are a riot of vivid colour.

*As autumn drifts into winter, the annual Round Table firework display is held in South Park,
popular with students and locals alike.*

*Headington Hill Park, one of Oxford's better-kept secrets, is at its most glorious bathed
in a rich autumnal light.*

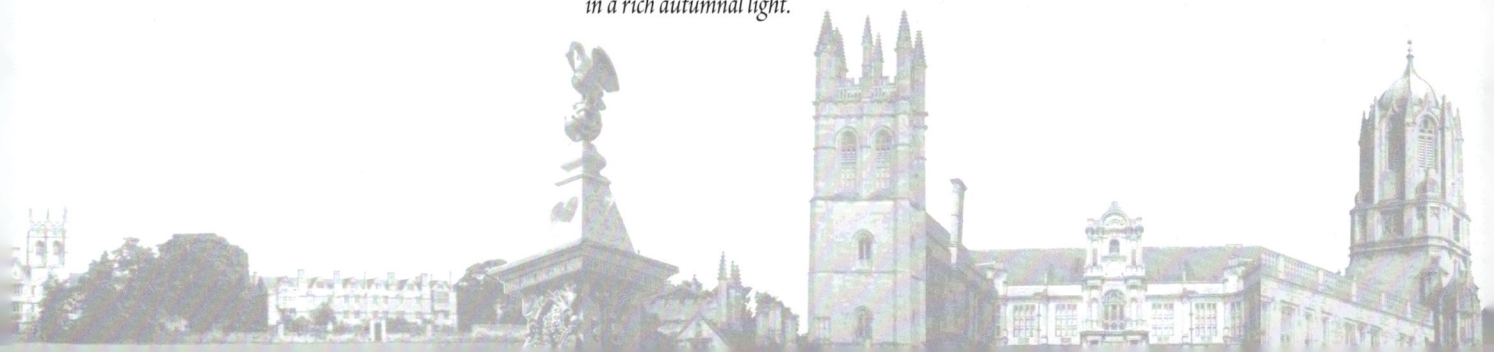

Michael Black, the sculptor who created the current 'emperors' heads, has indicated they may simply represent the history of fashion in facial hair!

One of the most arresting sights on Broad Street is the collection of sculptured heads surrounding the Sheldonian Theatre. While the identity of these bearded 'emperors' is a mystery, suggestions of who they represent range from Greek philosophers to Roman emperors to the Apostles. Originally commissioned by Wren and created by William Byrd in 1669, they were replaced in 1868 and again in the 1970s.

Oxford United began as a village football team in 1893. They have had a turbulent time of it: winning the Milk Cup in 1986 and in recent times, like many smaller clubs, struggling to keep afloat financially. The image on the club badge derives from the city arms – an 'ox' crossing a 'ford'.

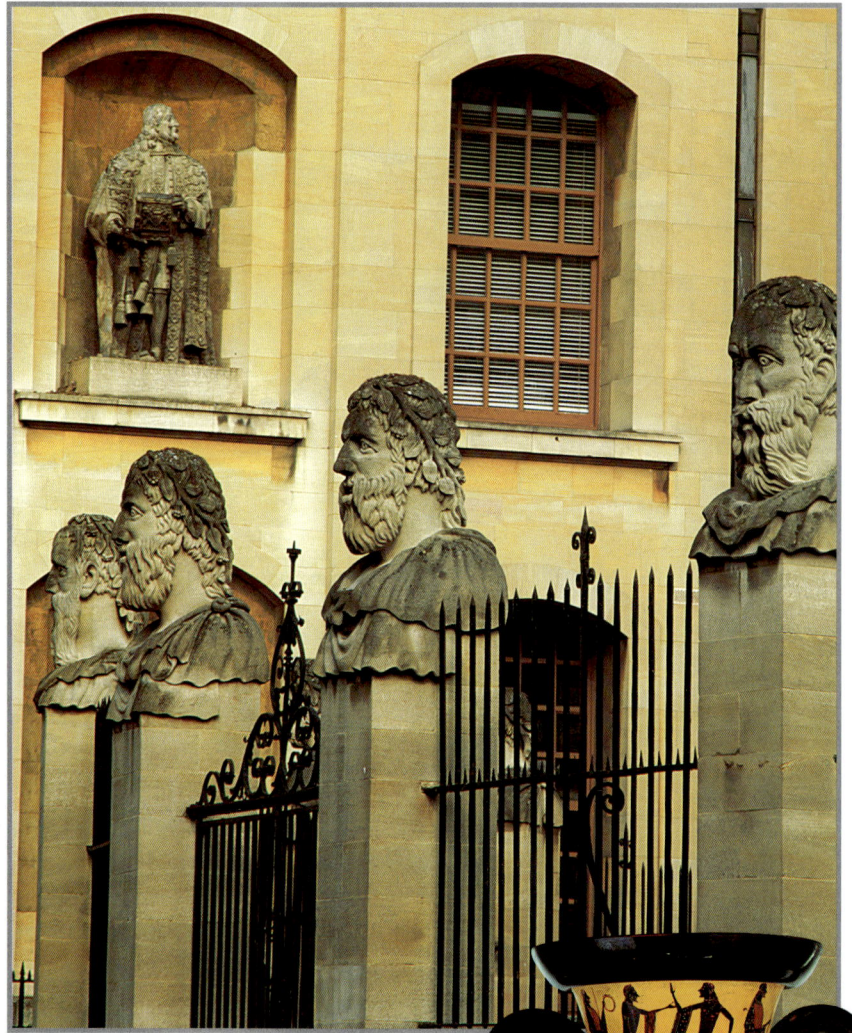

This amphora can be found in the Ashmolean Museum's Department of Antiquities and dates from the 6th–5th century BC. It depicts Hermes, the Greek messenger god with winged boots, bidding farewell to Zeus, the supreme god of Greek mythology.

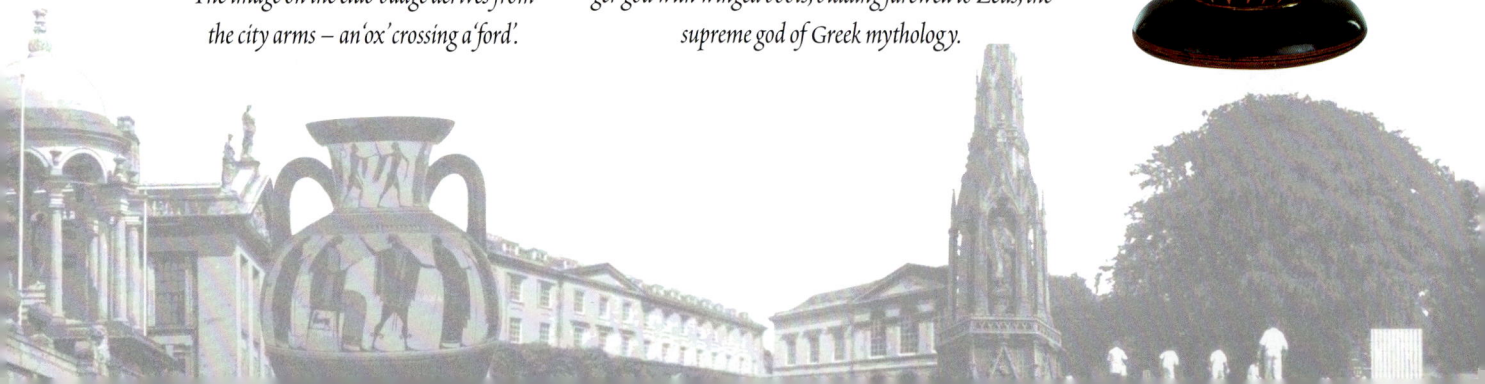

Medieval gargoyles and grotesques are often a fascinating blend of the comic and the ugly. Gargoyles have a practical function such as diverting water away from stone walls. Grotesques may have a moral function such as acting as a reminder of the transience of beauty or the folly of pride, they may have been intended to ward off evil, be merely decorative or be a combination of any of these. Grotesques can be found all over Oxford – this one gazes down from a Magdalen College wall.

The Pitt Rivers Museum is a fascinating, higgledy-piggledy collection of ethnographic and archaeological artefacts. This water snake with a dragon's head comes from Sarawak and represents a spirit thought to cause heart disease. A ritual is used to transfer the malady from the person to the image and the image is then placed in the river.

Perching on a stone sundial in the front quad of Corpus Christi College, a pelican pecks at her own breast in order to feed her young. A symbol of Christ's sacrifice, the pelican also appears on the college arms.

POSUI DEUM ADIUTOREM MEUM

EST REPOSITA JUSTITÆ CORONA

PRÆSIDE THOMA TURNER

At the feet of the statues of Walter de Merton and Henry III in the Merton College gate tower is a 15th-century relief depicting a woodland scene. It is thought to depict St John the Baptist in the wilderness, surrounded by birds, rabbits, bears and the symbolic lamb and unicorn.

A barber's pole is perhaps the most recognizable shop sign today, but at one time such signs were far more commonplace. The sign above Payne & Son, Silversmiths, on the High Street – a dog holding a watch in its mouth – is a reminder of this bygone age.

For many years a fox and three owls were kept at Corpus Christi in remembrance of the college's founders: Richard Fox and Bishop Hugh Oldham (pronounced Owldham).

A LITERARY LEGACY

In Alice's Adventures in Wonderland the dormouse mentions a 'treacle well' which refers to a surviving well at St Margaret's church, Binsey. Many pilgrims, including Henry VIII and Catherine of Aragon, visited the well in the past.

Alice Liddell used to come to this shop to buy barley sugar and Alice aficionados will recognize the Old Sheep Shop from Through the Looking-Glass. The shop now sells gifts and Alice memorabilia.

The Eastgate Hotel on the High Street was a favourite watering hole of the friends C.S. Lewis, who wrote The Chronicles of Narnia, *and J.R.R. Tolkien, who wrote* The Hobbit *and* The Lord of the Rings.

The picturesque Bridge of Sighs was built in 1913 and links the north and south sides of Hertford College. Like much of the college, the bridge was designed by T. G. Jackson and imitates its Venetian inspiration. The novelist Evelyn Waugh was at Hertford and his classic novel Brideshead Revisited recalls a golden under-graduate life in Oxford.

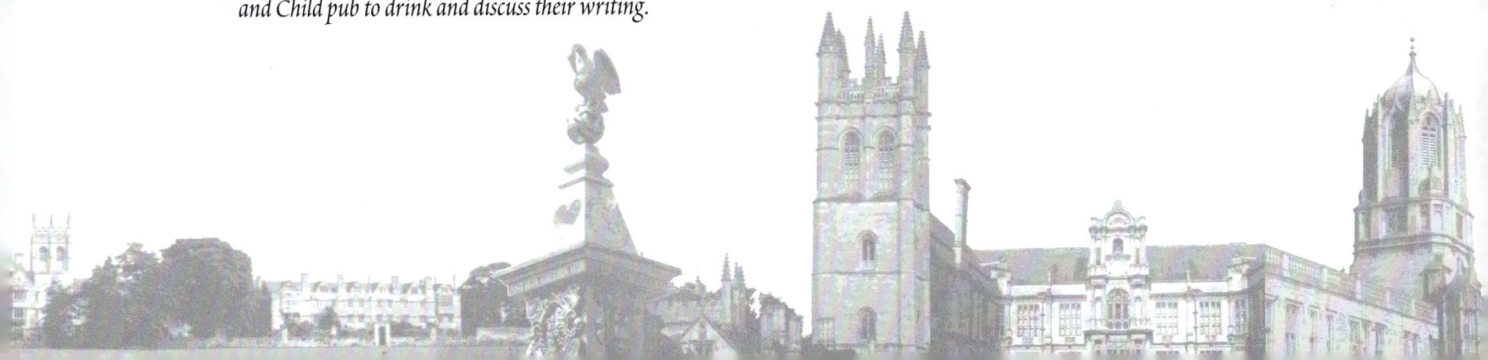

Lewis and Tolkien, together with the poet Charles Williams and other friends, formed a literary crowd known as the 'Inklings'. They met in the 'Rabbit Room' of The Eagle and Child pub to drink and discuss their writing.

When William Shakespeare travelled between London and Stratford he often broke his journey at the Crown Tavern, which confusingly stood across the road from the present Crown Inn on Cornmarket Street. In the 1920s, 16th-century wall paintings were discovered behind oak panelling in a room in which Shakespeare may have stayed. The Painted Room, at no. 3 Cornmarket Street, can be viewed by prior appointment with the building's occupants 'Oxford Aunts'.

The great dramatist Oscar Wilde had already gained a degree in Dublin when he moved into rooms overlooking the river at Magdalen in 1874. A keen supporter of the Aesthetic movement, Wilde became more flamboyant in speech and dress and decorated his rooms with objets d'art. Wilde's relationship with Lord Alfred Douglas ('Bosie'), who he met on a later visit to Oxford, was to lead to his eventual imprisonment and ruin, but Wilde retained a love of the city for the rest of his life.

Vera Brittain, the socialist author who wrote about her struggle for education, was taught at Somerville College. On 14 October 1920, Brittain and fellow writers Dorothy L. Sayers and Winifred Holtby were among the first women to receive degrees.

William Davenant, the playwright and poet, was the son of the landlord of the Crown Tavern and Shakespeare stood as William's godfather at a nearby church in 1606.

The first television adaptation of Colin Dexter's Inspector Morse novels was screened in the late 1980s. The series went on to become an undisputed success with John Thaw in the title role, Kevin Whately as the dependable Sergeant Lewis, and Oxford providing the exquisite locations.

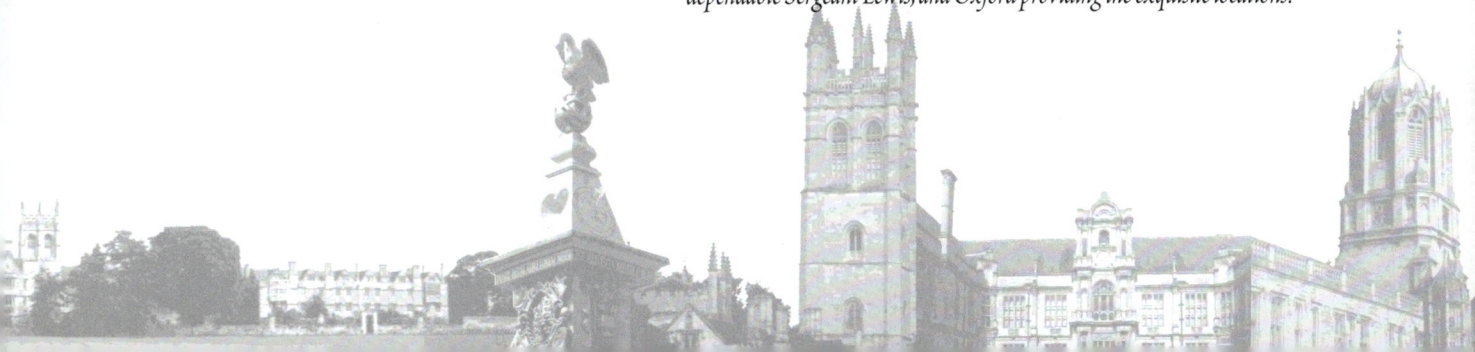

In 1966 Richard Burton and Elizabeth Taylor performed at the Oxford Playhouse free of charge, enabling the theatre to build a new extension: the Burton-Taylor Rooms.

Lovers of music will be familiar with the Sheldonian Theatre, which provides a fine setting for concerts as well as for the traditional university ceremonies and lectures. Designed by Wren, the Sheldonian has a mellow, classical exterior and a memorable interior with a superb canvas ceiling painted to suggest an open sky. Climb to the cupola at the top to be rewarded with unparalleled views over the city.

The Museum of Modern Art (MOMA) is tucked away in Pembroke Street and has an enviable reputation as a forum for contemporary work in all media. The MOMA café downstairs is a pleasant place to rest the feet and grab a bite.

The pillared façade of the Ashmolean Museum fronts a diverse collection of arte-facts including Guy Fawkes' lantern, the mantle of Pocahontas' father Powhattan and the Alfred Jewel. One of the museum's primary attractions is the Department of Western Art which includes drawings by Michelangelo and Raphael as well as works by Pre-Raphaelites and Impressionists.

The Bate Collection of Musical Instruments – a unique museum where many of the instruments are used – has a fascinating collection of historical European woodwind, brass and percussion instruments. Other treasures include items such as this, a single manual harpsichord (c. 1720) which may have belonged to G. F. Handel.

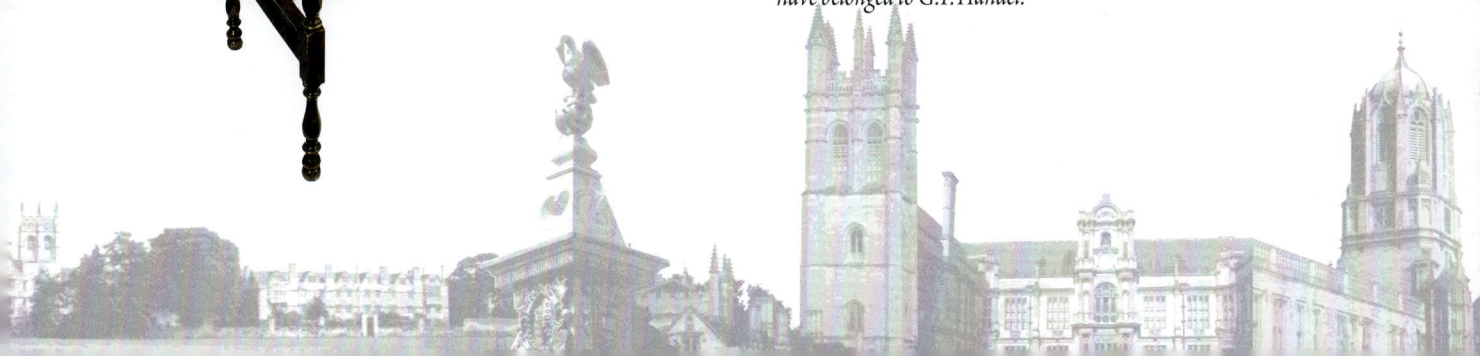

In how many city centres do you find a herd of deer living just off the High Street? About 40 fallow deer are kept in Magdalen Grove Deer Park, one for each of the college's original Fellows.

Deadman's Walk, which runs behind Merton College, was in medieval times the processional route to the Jewish cemetery, now the Botanic Garden.

The graceful 'Rainbow' Bridge in the University Parks was built in 1923 as a public work intended to alleviate unemployment. Funded by the city, university, colleges and individuals, it represents a rare level of cooperation between town and gown. The bridge provides a sublime viewpoint from which to gaze at the tranquillity of the parks, while ducks and punts drift below.

Originally punts were used as working craft – for fishing, transporting and delivering. The Victorians preserved the practice of punting by using punts as leisure boats. Today, punting is almost confined to Oxford and Cambridge. In Oxford the tradition is to punt from the slope, but in Cambridge, to punt from the deck end.

The Botanic Garden was founded by Henry Danvers, Earl Danby, as part of the School of Medicine in 1621. The Doric arch that faces the High Street was built in 1633 and features a bust of Earl Danby as well as statues of Charles I and Charles II in the attire of Roman emperors. The Botanic Garden in Oxford is the oldest physic garden in Britain and the third oldest in the world.

*South Park sits alongside a busy road that runs from St Clements up
the hill to Headington but it is a wonderful spot within the city from
which to view the majestic 'dreaming spires'.*

A detour off the busy High Street or St Aldate's can lead you to one of Oxford's most tranquil green spaces – Christ Church Meadow. You can approach the meadow through either the War Memorial Gardens or a turnstile behind the Head of the River pub on St Aldate's or from Rose Lane or Merton Street. Broad Walk provides impressive views of Christ Church, Merton and Magdalen tower and Poplar Walk leads to the river.

Slightly off the beaten track from the majority of the colleges is Worcester, at the bottom of Beaumont Street. A tunnel at the end of the medieval cottages leads you to the beautiful gardens, an image borrowed by Lewis Carroll when he described the tunnel and garden Alice found when she fell down the rabbit hole. Today you can take a walk around the lake where the real Alice used to feed the ducks.

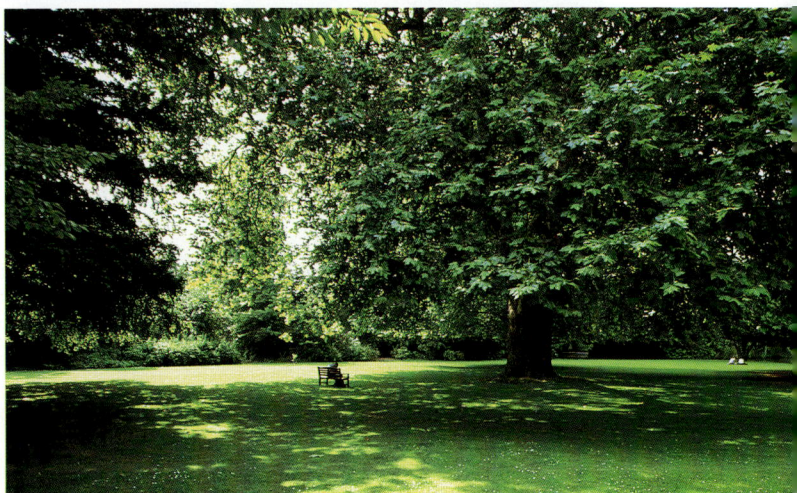

One of the beauties of Oxford is the large amount of green space in so relatively small a city. Port Meadow, stretching from west of Jericho to Wolvercote, is an ancient expanse of pastureland that was mentioned in the Domesday Book of 1087 and has never been ploughed.

Once a year, on an unspecified day, the Sheriff of Oxford rounds up the animals on Port Meadow and fines the owners of those grazing illegally.

MESSING ABOUT IN BOATS

Punting is part of the summer in Oxford. Hire a punt from Magdalen Bridge or from the Cherwell Boathouse in North Oxford, take a picnic and spend a day messing about on the river.

Iffley Lock is mentioned in Jerome K. Jerome's classic comic novel Three Men in a Boat.

The Trout Inn at Wolvercote enjoys a picturesque setting beside the River Thames (known as the River Isis in Oxford). Originally a fisherman's cottage, it is pleasant in summer as the call of the peacocks echoes over the river and in winter when the interior is made cosy by roaring fires.

The Head of the River is Oxford's largest pub and was a former wharf house of neighbouring Salters the boat builders. From Salters you can take a boat trip to historic Abingdon. The pub owes its name to the city's rowing tradition. The rowing team or 'eight' tries to bump the one in front, thus moving up a place. The team that wins is said to be head of the river.

Folly Bridge is thought to be the site of the original oxen-ford or crossing point over the Thames.

Picturesque narrowboats are a familiar sight, such as this one near Folly Bridge.

AT WORK AND PLAY

Visitors often find the idea of the university – with no central campus – confusing. They discover it to be a diverse mixture of colleges, some rich, some comparatively poor, some with a reputation for academic excellence and some with a proud sporting history. Each of the colleges has its own personality and traditions and students associate themselves with their college rather than with their faculty.

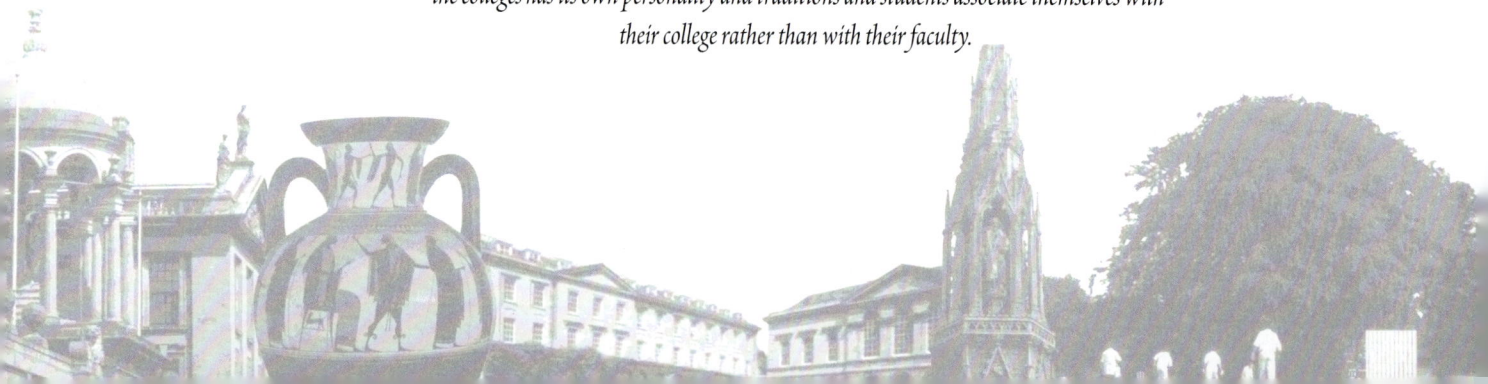

The Turf Tavern is a popular pub tucked away between Holywell Street and New College Lane. It is reached by either of two winding alleyways, Bath Place or St Helen's Passage. The latter, formerly Hell Passage, was a miserable back street in the 1850s and was the home of Jane Burden, later Jane Morris, and the face of much Pre-Raphaelite art. Having been spotted by Rossetti and Burne-Jones, she became Rossetti's and also William Morris' model. She and William were married at St Michael at the North Gate but Rossetti was always infatuated with her and her face appears on many of his works.

Students and locals alike choose to relax in the University Parks in the summer. And as familiar a sight as punts on the Cherwell, is that of a game of cricket. The Oxford University Cricket Club plays county and international sides and has produced top players in the past, including Imran Khan and Colin Cowdrey.

The Bear, one of Oxford's oldest pubs, has a collection of over 5,000 ties –

so if you go for a drink wearing an unusual one – beware!

The King's Arms on the corner of Parks Road and Holywell Street is a favourite with students, particularly when they are celebrating the end of their exams. A coaching inn in the 18th century, the pub has been quenching the thirsts of academics and travellers since 1607.

Students clustering around the Examination Schools on the High Street are a common sight in June. To sit their exams, students must dress in 'subfusc' – a formal outfit in black and white with gowns.

BEYOND OXFORD

The land on which Blenheim Palace stands was a gift from Queen Anne to John Churchill, 1st Duke of Marlborough, as a reward for military success and was intended to be a testament of Britain's supremacy. The architecture was the extravagant creation of John Vanbrugh and Hawksmoor, and the beautiful park was landscaped by 'Capability' Brown.

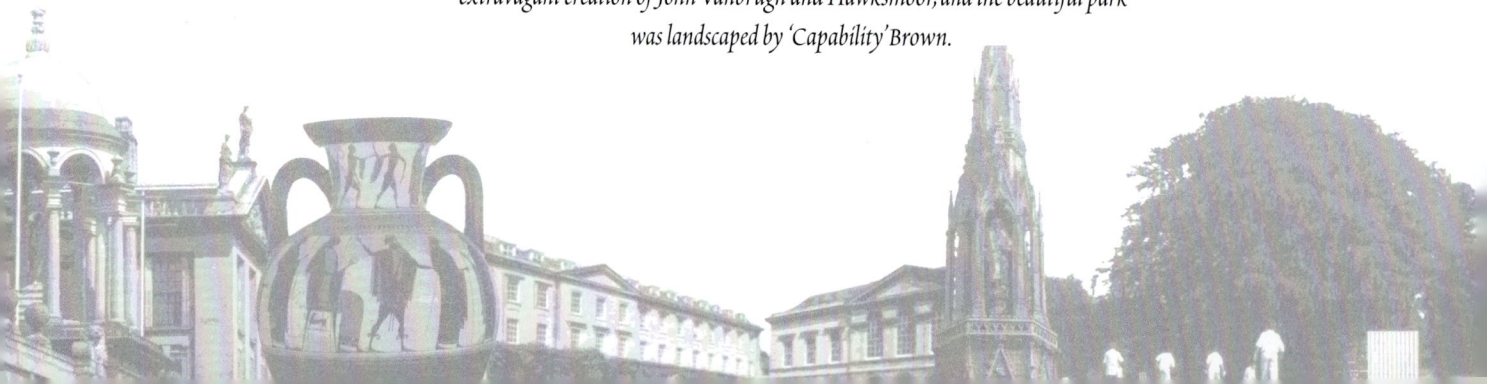

The prehistoric Rollright Stones at Great Rollright comprise three groups: the solitary King Stone, the circle known as the King's Men, and the Whispering Knights, thought to form part of an ancient burial chamber. According to legend, the number of stones in the mysterious circle cannot be counted.

The serene landscaped garden of Rousham Park House has been little altered since it was created by William Kent in the 18th century. The walled garden with its pigeon house, espalier fruit trees, and enchanting herbaceous borders is a delight.

Winston Churchill was born at Blenheim Palace and proposed to Clementine, his future wife, in the Temple of Diana. They are buried at the nearby church of Bladon.

Broughton Castle, the home of Lord and Lady Saye and Sele, has been a family home for over six centuries. Enclosed by a broad moat, Broughton has a medieval Great Hall, a fine collection of arms and armour, and splendid panelling and plaster ceilings. During the English Civil War, Broughton Castle was the setting for secret meetings of Parliamentary leaders. More recently, it provided a glorious backdrop to the Oscar-winning film Shakespeare in Love.

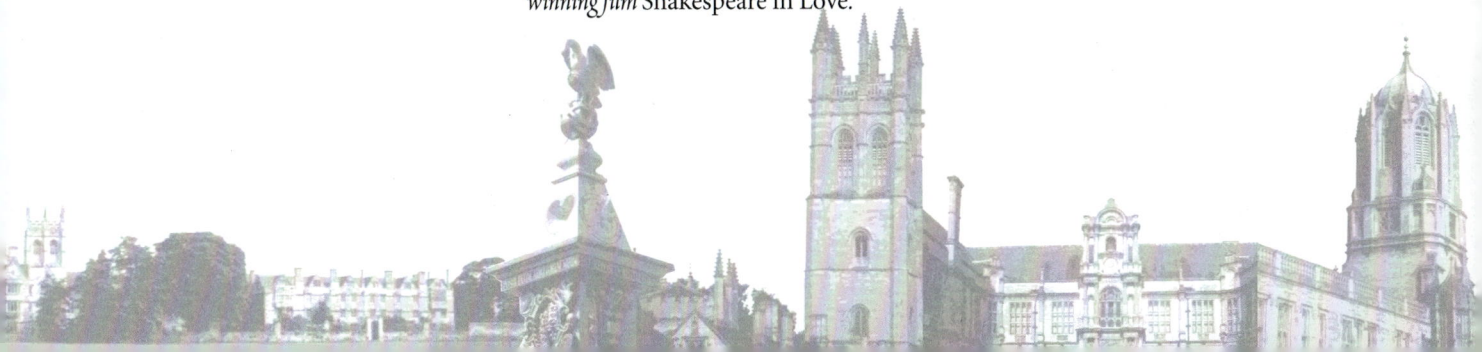

*Favourite destinations for families include the Cotswold Wildlife Park, near Burford,
and the Cotswold Farm Park, the headquarters of the Rare Breeds Survival Trust.*

*Cogges Manor Farm Museum near Witney explores rural life in the county in the Victo-
rian period. There is plenty to interest younger visitors, including sampling home baking
from the kitchen, playing games and meeting the farmyard animals.*

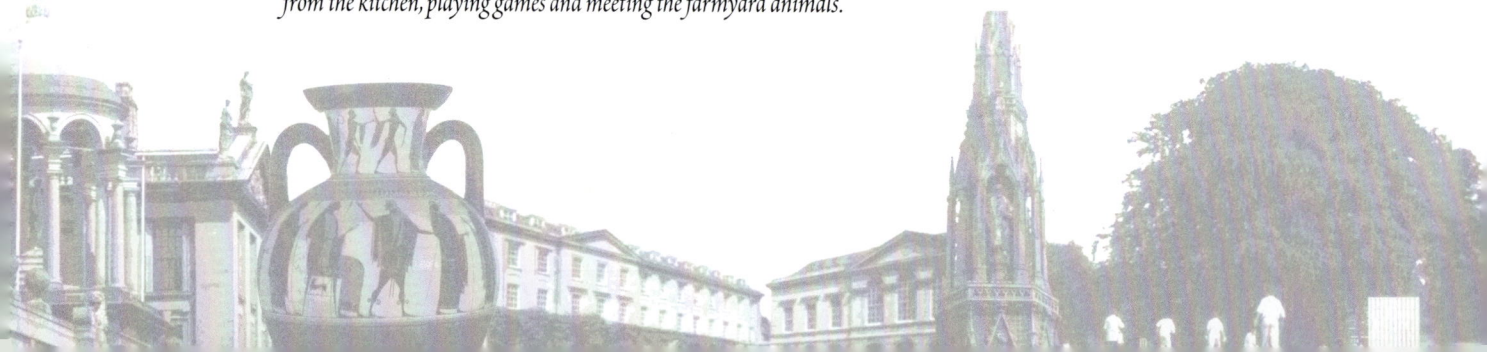

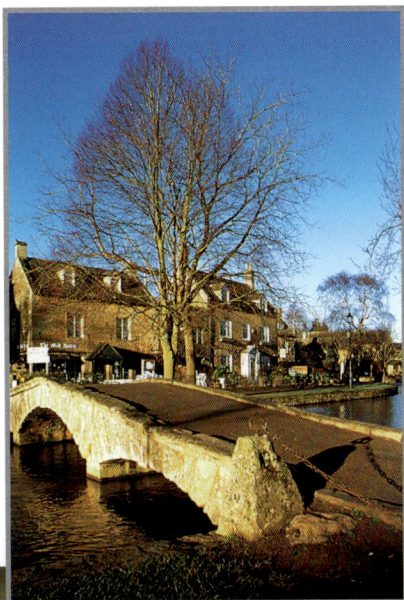

Bourton-on-the-Water is one of the most popular Cotswold villages with visitors, home to a model village, a motor museum, a model railway and Birdland.

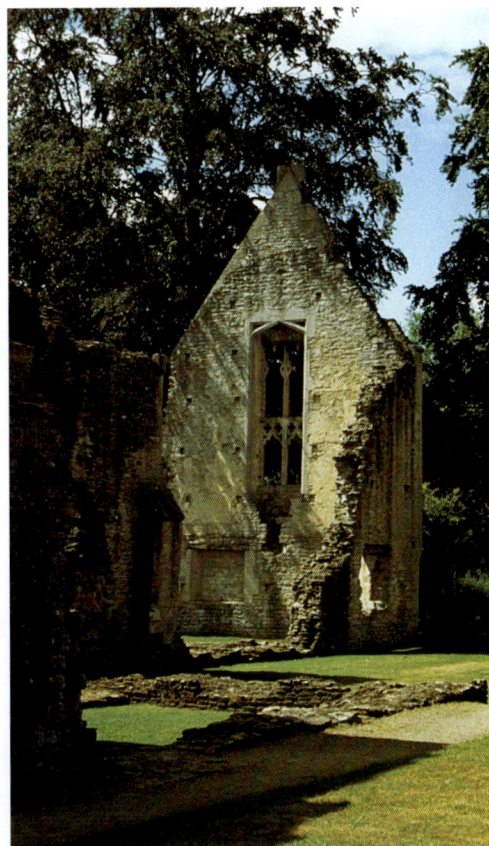

William Morris' bedroom at Kelmscott Manor, near Lechlade, Gloucestershire, with 17th-century oak four-poster bed and embroideries by Jane and May Morris. A compulsory visit for devotees of William Morris, Kelmscott was the house Morris fell in love with and shared with his family and Dante Gabriel Rossetti.

The River Windrush provides a serene backdrop to the ruins of Minster Lovell Hall, but this 15th-century manor house is linked with an eerie legend. It is said that Francis Lovell, an influential man who fought for Richard III during the Wars of the Roses – and now with a price on his head – returned home in secret. Notifying just one servant so that he could be fed each day, he hid in a locked underground chamber. The legend tells that somehow the plan failed; in the 18th century workmen discovered the skeleton of a man, sitting at a table – presumably the missing Francis Lovell.

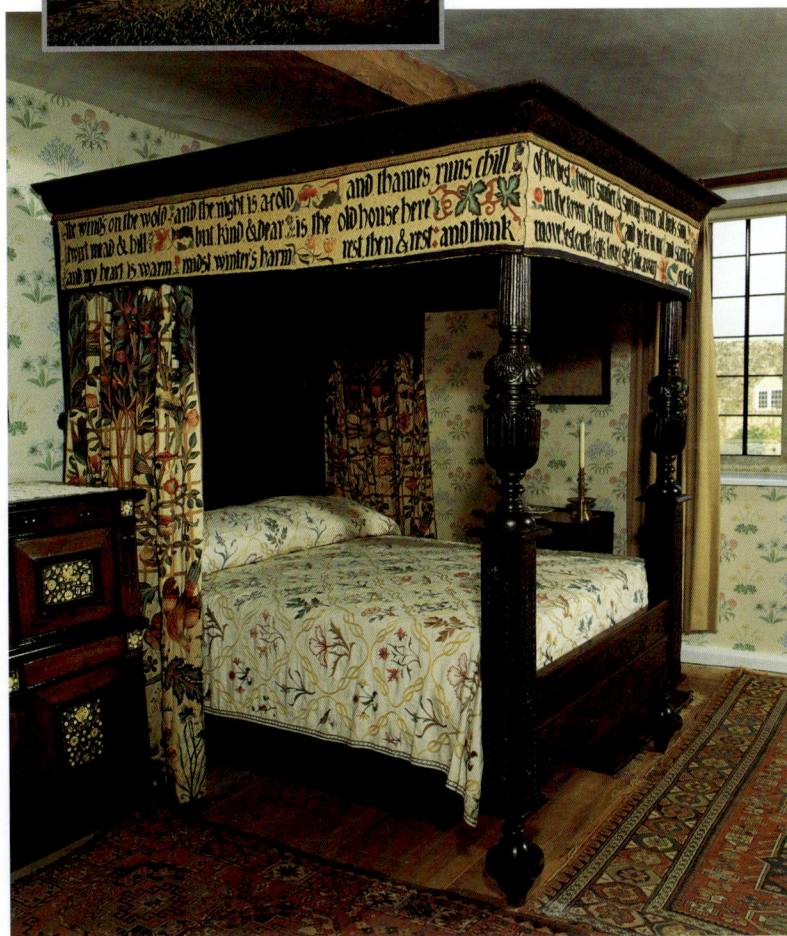

Greys Court, near Henley-on-Thames, is a charming 16th-century house built beside the ruins of a medieval castellated manor. The house is lived in so, although only the ground floor is on view to the public, has a real sense of a home. There are charming gardens and the outbuildings include a Tudor donkey wheel, a horse wheel and a 19th-century ice house.

The world-famous Royal Regatta has been held at Henley-on-Thames since 1839. Every July, the people who want to see and be seen flock to Henley to enjoy what is not just a sporting occasion, but an essential date on the social calendar.

The Great Western Society has recreated the golden age of steam at Didcot Railway Centre. Enthusiasts can inspect the carefully restored collection in the engine shed and ride in a 1930s steam train.

According to legend, travellers who left their horses and a silver coin by Wayland's Smithy would find the horses shod on their return.

What are the origins of the mysterious chalk carving on White Horse Hill? Some say it was created to honour King Alfred's victory over the Danes, some that it dates back to the Bronze Age. A walk from White Horse Hill along the ancient Ridgeway leads you to Wayland's Smithy, a 5,000-year-old burial chamber named after a Saxon god.

Sulgrave Manor is a fine example of a manor house during the time of Shakespeare and a reminder of the relationship between Britain and the United States. It was home to the ancestors of George Washington from 1539 for over a century.

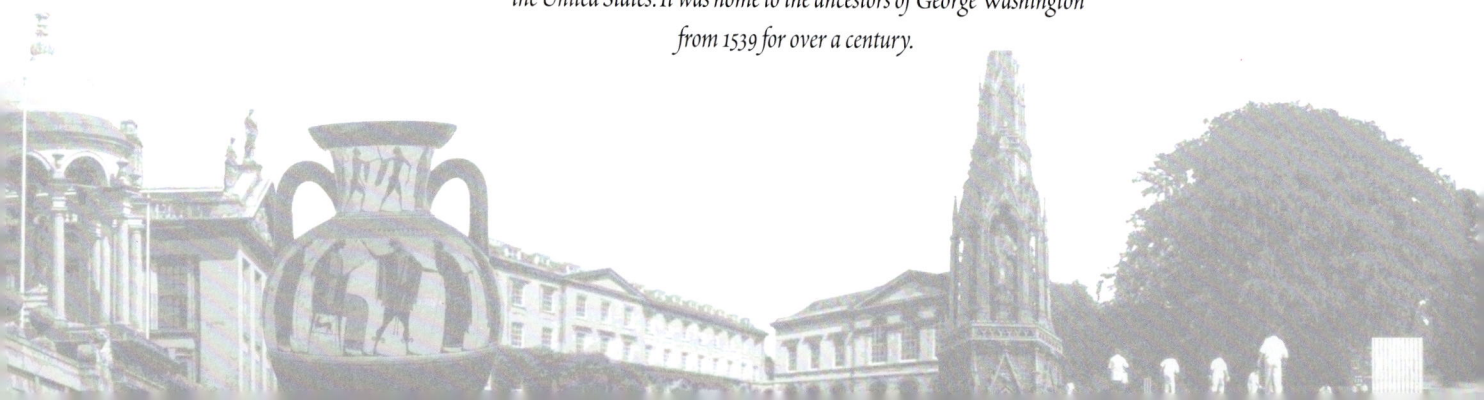

To the northeast of Oxford lies Brill, a hill and a windmill. On fine, breezy days plenty of families come to fly kites and enjoy the view.

Waddesdon Manor, near Aylesbury, Buckinghamshire, was built for Baron Ferdinand de Rothschild in the style of a French Renaissance chateau. The house boasts an excellent collection of 18th-century French decorative art, while the garden includes a Victorian parterre, a Rococo aviary and a Children's Garden Trail.

During the Reformation Stonor Park became a centre of Catholic thought, members of the family were penalized for their beliefs and a secret room in the roof housed the martyr Edmund Campion.

Stonor Park, a family home for eight centuries, has stained glass, fine furniture and paintings.

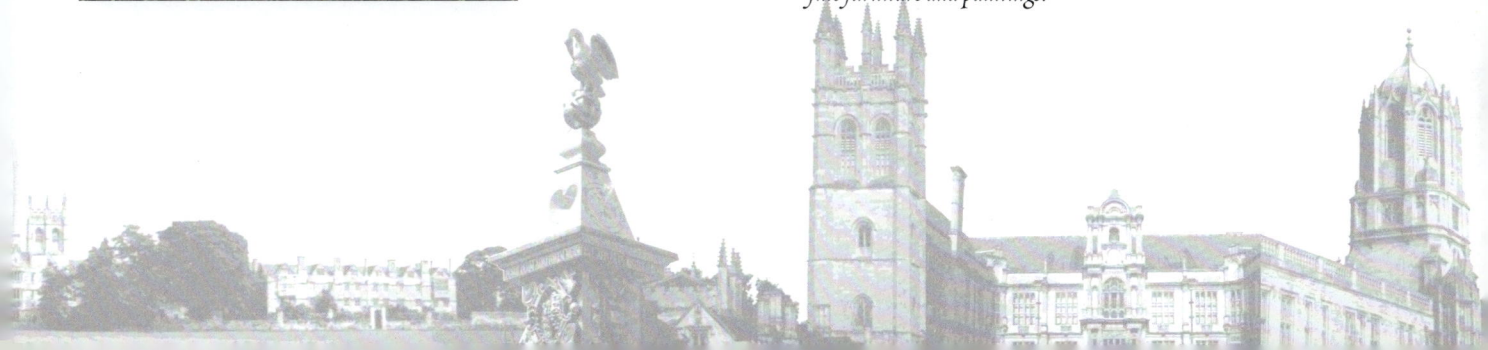

INDEX